The First Noble Truth

The First Noble Truth

Poems by

Steve Kowit

UNIVERSITY OF TAMPA PRESS
TAMPA, FLORIDA

Manufactured in the United States of America
Printed on acid-free paper ∞
First Edition

On the Cover: "Patriarch Monk and Tiger." Attributed to Shi Ke. Courtesy of Tokyo National Museum. Image: TNM Image Archives Source: http://TnmArchives.jp/

Special thanks to Christian and Faye Hayashi and to Satoko Aida for their assistance with permission to reproduce this extraordinary tenth-century work of art.

The University of Tampa Press
401 West Kennedy Boulevard
Tampa, FL 33606

ISBN 978-159732-025-2 (hbk.)
ISBN 978-159732-026-9 (pbk.)

Browse & order online at
http://utpress.ut.edu

Library of Congress Cataloging-in-Publication Data

Kowit, Steve.
   The first noble truth : poems by / Steve Kowit. -- 1st ed.
      p. cm.
   ISBN 978-1-59732-025-2 (hardback : alk. paper) -- ISBN 978-1-59732-026-9 (pbk. : alk. paper)
   I. Title.
   PS3561.O87F57 2007
   811'.54--dc22   2006103105

Contents

No Turning Back

That Ecstasy of Kisses

That Other Life

For Mary, of course;
in memory of my beloved parents;
for the spirit of Rachel Corrie;
for the international resistance;
and for my teachers Quan Yin & Mullah Nasruddin.

Reader, calm yourself: I am no agent of discord, no firebrand of sedition. I anticipate history by a few days.

Pierre-Joseph Proudhon

No Turning Back

Snapshot

At night, a man is sitting at his desk in pain, aging,
full of fears & dreams, till Jesse barges in
& nuzzles his left leg & says, Hey,
you know that open box of Milk Bones
in the kitchen? Well, I've been thinking . . .
The man washes down another Vicodin,
scratches the dog's head, & the two of them
get up & leave the room. When he returns,
he sees how dark it is outside, & late.
He types & stops, looking for a phrase he can't
quite find, some gesture that the past
had given him & taken back.
Above his desk, that ancient snapshot of his folks,
two Lower East Side kids, their lives together
just beginning, who will never understand
that everything the future holds for them
has passed. Dexter Gordon's hushed
& melancholic take on "Don't Explain" drifts
quietly across the room, as if that saxophone
knew, somehow, that the fellow staring
at that photo had been weeping, stupidly
& over nothing. At the keyboard, Sonny Clark
looks over once at Dex & nods, & shuts
his eyes, & listens to himself—to both of them.
Staring out the window at the dark,
the man finds, he thinks, at last,
what he's been looking for, & goes on typing.

Little Miss Broadway

1938 & it's official—Norma Shearer will play Scarlett O'Hara.
Hit by an aerial torpedo, the freighter Thorpeness
burns & sinks outside Valencia Harbor.
Joe Louis takes down Max Schmelling with a ribroaster,
five lightning hooks & a right to the jaw.
Mott's Apple Juice hits the American market.
The Imperial Navy moves up the Yangtze to Matang.
In Paris, Herschel Grynzpan shoots Ernst vom Rath.
The Kristallnacht Riots erupt. Superman, in his debut,
hoists a green car over his head. Neville Chamberlain
signs a non-aggression pact with the Reich assuring peace
in our time. On Thursday, June 30th, while Stéphane Grappelli
& Django Reinhardt record *Limehouse Blues* at the Hot
Club in Paris, Billie Kowit, née Ginsburg, gives birth to a son.
At Pimlico, Seabiscuit beats War Admiral by four lengths.
The Nuremberg Laws clamp shut their teeth
on the throats of the Romani people & Jews.
The exterminations begin—Nuremberg, which gave us
the clock with the toothed wheel. In front of a wax museum
statue of Mussolini, Epiphani Dante raises a pistol
to his temple & fires. Austria joins the Reich. The Sudetenland
is annexed. Decca releases Ella Fitzgerald's *This
Time It's Real*. Shirley Temple stars in *Little Miss Broadway*.

An Education

Your first day of school:
Mother kisses your forehead,
slips her hand out of yours,
whirls you about,
& gives you a gentle shove
into the future.
Clutching your lunchpail
you stumble into the classroom,
not without apprehension.
There is your seat
& there are the wooden alphabet blocks,
& there is your teacher
who sits at her desk
without moving,
her hair blowing in every direction,
her eyes open wide
& her mouth open too
& a fly on her nose.
She is dead.
You leap to your feet, shrieking,
your eyes squinched up tight
& your fists to your ears,
but the other kids
tell you to shush up
or you'll get them all into trouble.
Apparently they have already grown
used to this peculiar
system of education.
& soon you will too.
A diligent & obedient student,
you will sit at your desk,
dead teacher or not,
& open your book,
& begin your lesson.

That Dog

we saw behind the hospital when I got out,
all agitated, racing back and forth along the fence,
clumps of hair pulled out in ugly patches,
had been waiting—now of course I understand
it—to be dragged off to some basement lab
where they would strap him to a table
& then slice his tongue out of his mouth,
or snip the cerebellum from its stem,
or set him flaming like a torch
in one of those burn research protocols
the NIH delights to grant.
He wagged his tail at us & through the chain-link
tried to lick my hand. Kneeling
outside the fence, I said: *Hey, buddy,
how's it going?*—assured him everything
was perfectly okay, & then walked on.
We hardly knew each other then.
Twice, you had been kind enough to visit me.
Up there, on Buena Vista Hill, crossing Parnassus,
I took your hand for the first time: the two of us
already half in love, & pleased, as lovers are,
with everything: the heart unwavering,
the day spun out of light, our human
brethren trustworthy & good. Ourselves
enraptured & oblivious,
unconscionably innocent & young.

A Betrayal

A friend I hadn't seen in more than three decades wrote
to tell me he had just remarried & was finally happy:
this followed by a long denunciation of his former wife,
whom I had known back then when all of us were young,
& who, through tireless manipulation & deceit (or so
he claimed), had won full custody of the kids,
thus ruining two decades of his life. "She wouldn't
even show me the room where they slept," he wrote,
"or offer me a cup of water from the kitchen tap."
I was shocked, though at the same time could not help
but think back to that afternoon a few weeks
after their first son's birth when my friend had dropped by,
exuberantly happy, & in the midst of kidding about how
little sleep they were getting, mentioned, in passing,
that they had taken Sasha, their lovable Irish setter,
back to the pound: "With an infant in the house . . ." he started
to explain—the way one might about a troublesome TV
or a sofabed returned for taking too much space up in the den.
I stood there stunned. "But . . . why . . . didn't you find her another
home?" I tried to keep my voice under control.
"You know as well as I do at those places only puppies
get adopted. She'll . . . she'll be put down."
It came out broken. I could hardly wrap my mouth
about the words. "Oh, not at all," he laughed. "Sasha's
so adorable she's bound to find a family that will take her in!"
He shook his head with a dismissive grin & then went on
about the endless pleasures of his infant son, & I said
nothing further. What more, I'd like to know, could I have said?
By the time I was done reading his letter, the sun had set.
I sat there for a long moment, then read it through
a second time, trying, this time, to be as careful as I could
not to betray our friendship, to keep in mind what a fine,
decent, well-intentioned fellow he had always been, & all

that he had evidently suffered. Though it didn't work. Sasha
kept pacing back and forth across the cage of that
disquieting letter, pausing now & then to lick the back
of my right hand. She could not comprehend what had happened.
Had she done something wrong? Where were those humans
she had loved so much, those humans who had seemed
so trustworthy & generous & kind? I folded up his letter,
set it down, & watched through the west window bands
of violet & magenta spread across the summer dusk & darken.
Try as I might, however earnestly I wish him well in his new life,
it smolders in me still—that old, unspoken, unforgiving anger.

The First Noble Truth

They loved *Siddhartha*. No surprises there! But when I pick up
the chalk & scratch on the board *DUKKA: The First
Noble Truth: Suffering permeates life*, no one looks pleased.
After a moment of general grumbling Marie Elena
mumbles aloud: *I'm not sure that's true.* Then Deegan
pipes in, *Buddha Deluda*—& that breaks the ice & everyone
laughs. But a laugh with an edge, a laugh that buzzes
around the room the way damaged wires back in the walls
sizzle before they're ready to blow. Then Carlos Padilla leaps
to his feet & says: *Suffering? Hell, no! That's just the crud
you wipe from your hands,* mendrugos *you shake from your hair!
This life is joy to the max! Just padding around in bare feet,
or sipping an icy Fanta, or sprawling out on the grass doing
lunch with a couple of homies.* . . . Feisty, full of exuberant health
& good looks & high spirits, Carlos defending our common lot
with such good-natured, passionate faith even I can't help
but grin, cheering him on. When he's done with that funny harangue,
almost everyone laughs. Half a dozen start clapping. But others
remain unconvinced. It's there on their faces: some of the older
ones in the back of the room, & Sean & Ty—& Ahmad for sure.
While the ones filled with the pleased, undauntable juices of life
are clapping & laughing, these others smile uneasily, discomforted,
silent. . . . Bradley stares at the back of his hand. Grace Huerta
listens politely, stroking her long, gray, beautiful hair. To my left,
the clock on the wall is much too insistently ticking away. Time
to stop all this chatter, time to release the slew of us back
into this piercingly rapturous, inexplicably marvelous world—world
that is everywhere freighted with sorrow. *Dukka*: the First Noble Truth.

The Burro

That little plaster donkey we had bought while waiting
at the San Ysidro-Tijuana border crossing years ago
was—but for the burnt umber they had painted her—
a perfect likeness of those burros climbing thru the mist-bound
mountains of Chiapas, bundles of firewood lashed
to their backs & their slender necks bowed slightly
in the harness: unhappy servants of the people
who had built Copan, carved Palenque, plotted the ecliptic
for a thousand years before the pious Spanish Christians
came to swing them from the trees & steal their land. At dawn,
each week, indians from Tenejapa & San Juan Chamula
would trot out of the hills, pack animals themselves,
hunched under bundles of *leña* & *carbon.*
One family or another would tap timorously at the door
of our adobe house in San Cristobal, & I'd open it & nod:
Si, bueno, yes, of course! & grateful & relieved they'd ease
the tumplines from their brows & slide those heavy
bundles from their backs & then unload the patient, small, dust-
colored burro who'd be standing by them in the courtyard,
dutiful & somber & resigned. Half the night they had been
climbing down those rocky mountain footpaths through the dark.
Not just grown men but women & young kids, many of them
barefoot, buffered from the cold in nothing but those threadbare
black *chamarras*, & we would pay for all that wood & charcoal
with a few measly pesos & a handful of tortillas.
With a crack, like the lash of a whip, that little souvenir
shop burro shattered one spring morning of her own weight,
shards of chalky plaster scattering beneath the picture
window where she'd stood, who silently, for years, had been
a keepsake to us of that other life—long-suffering servant
of the servants of the Mexican sierra: that little plaster burro
at the window in the light, by the blue ceramic bell from Tuxtla,
& the black Oaxacan flute, & the African violets, & the wandering Jew.

The Erased

Inside this pencil
crouch words that have never been written!
                    W. S. Merwin

Bill, how on earth could you think that those marvelous
unwritten words would be lurking around in just any old pencil?
Hell no, they're only in one. & it just so happens
that I'm the lucky fellow who's got it! Yup—me! That's right.
Incredible as it may seem, I just have to touch that pencil to paper
& presto! A perfect poem every time!
Enchanting . . . melodic . . . unsurpassably deft.
Every least phoneme flawlessly balanced & wrought!
Not a figure that isn't exquisite & telling!
Each syllable ringing the orphic bell of the soul!
Believe me, Bill, I would have rushed off a sample at once,
only . . . well, as it turns out, the thing was designed sort of funny:
not straight up & down like your normal, everyday pencil,
but curved in an arc so that perfect eraser, brushing after each letter,
wipes everything out the instant it's written, leaving the page
as blank & bereft as the void. You can imagine my horror—
having to watch the loveliest verse in the language dissolve
from the page & vanish forever. I'll spare you
my unappeasable anguish. The rage & despair.
Suffice it to say, in the end, I have come to some
sort of uneasy peace with the whole unfortunate business,
understanding at last what should have been clear from the start—
that even more than that fabulous pencil itself
it's that fiendish eraser—unwriting everything back into silence—
that makes it, when all's said & done,
the very last word in both verisimilitude & perfection.

A Mania

A mania for kabbalism, witchery, candles & black lace.
A preoccupation with omens & signs: Salvation,
End Time, the Rapture, the frenzy of being possessed
by the ministrations of Satan. Compulsive attraction
to pentagrams, yarrow sticks, amulets, divination
by firelight. Devotional excitation of crowds.
Delusion that incubi inhabit one's body. A lust for tattoos,
frottage, a hunger to speak with the dead.
Uncontrollable impulse toward self-mutilation,
a craving to pick open wounds, that erotomaniacal urge
to make love in a Pullman hurtling over the countryside
in a thundering downpour at midnight, as you & I
had once so elaborately planned—that teeming,
convulsive need that for years I was haunted
& plagued by. Delirious, insurmountable hunger
—mumbling & weeping your name—of which
nothing could cure me & nothing diminish: chain
of insatiable shuddering sleeper cars banging
& screaming into that dark, driving, doomed, impossible rain.

Marilyn, A Confabulation

*Marilyn's death was one of those news events about which you
can remember how you heard it, where you heard it, and how
you felt.*

Charles Champlin, *The Los Angeles Times*

Three weeks before we called it quits, Marilyn & I had caught the subway
to Naponsett Beach, & picking up a *New York Daily News*
discarded on the seat beside us, read that in her Brentwood,
California, home, Marilyn Monroe had swallowed pills & killed herself.
Everything became at once immensely vivid, the way it feels
when you step from a darkened theater into the astonishing
glare of an ordinary afternoon, & for two or three minutes that all
but unbearable light is at once thrilling & painful to move through.
Though it's possible, I suppose, given that it was so many decades back,
that I'm misremembering. For all I know it was nothing but the shimmer
of that August sunlight off the ocean that has gotten mixed up
with my feelings. You know how it is when such a day detaches
itself from the days around it, which I suppose is why I think
that I remember it so clearly: Marilyn & I lying on that beach,
the frightful pounding of enormous waves, & how she looked at me:
that elfin, mischievous expression as I bent to press my lips
against her mouth. Listen, I know as well as anyone how
hopelessly confused such memories get, & that a poem like this
comes out of nothing but a kind of self-indulgent tenderness
for one's own history: a longing to reclaim that woman, decades back,
whom I had stupidly let slip out of my life. Then too, everything
—the fragrance of her flesh, that blanket's scent, the irrepressible
expression on her face as I bent toward her, that prodigious
tide—might well be all mixed up with fugitive & half-connected
images of other women, beaches, summers, that unhappy
movie goddess who had killed herself, some quirk of light
reflected off the sand, with nothing but nostalgia
for my own youth, some longing, less for her than for the infinite.

[13]

All that aside, that afternoon, though forty-some-odd years ago,
is with me still: Marilyn's impossibly seductive look,
all witchery & provocation as she lay beside me
on the scorching sand. Naponsett Beach: the sun ablaze
above the North Atlantic shelf, the ocean's seawrack-salted air
laced with that narcotic heat. & at our feet, immense, tumultuous—
even now I'd swear to it—the dark, percussive thunder of those breakers.

The Bus to Pomasqui

Then it was settled—I'd cut myself loose from a life
as fetid & tangled as sea wrack
& start again where nobody knew me. I dug out
my maps & circled the likeliest spot: Pomasqui.
Directly on the equator. Latitude zero. Yeah,
that would do nicely. Stuffing what little I owned
in my green canvas sack I trekked my way south
to Cali, then Guayaquil up to Quito
where somebody told me what bus I should catch
—which I did. We lurched from the stop with a screech.
Thrown off my feet, I flailed about till I managed,
somehow, to grab at a strap & tumble into a seat.
When I looked out the window the city was gone.
The Andean landscape rushed past, exquisite
perhaps, but quicker than one would have guessed.
That fool was gunning us over those hills
at incredible speeds. I gasped as I stared at the man
at the wheel: immense, obese, his head
oddly misshapen, his massive neck varnished
in sweat. The face in his rear-view mirror, the sort
that one sees in asylums—without any forehead
to speak of & eyes much too small & too far apart.
I was scared. Scared out of my wits. Outside,
what must have been mountains & rivers flew by
in a blur. The sun, like something too leaden to float,
tore heavily thru the horizon. Then night,
with its flickering shadows, & now & again
in the distance the lights of what must have been cities.
No doubt the town of Pomasqui among them.
"Pomasqui!" I cried out as I leapt to my feet.
But the bus bucked, slamming me back. We weren't
going to stop, that much was clear. "Now see here!
See here!" I screamed out as loud as I dared—

which is when I saw what I should have seen
from the start: the man had no ears. I started to weep.
"It's not fair! It's simply not fair!" —The others,
stolid & silent *Ecuadoreños*, sat wrapped
in their ponchos, unmoving. I sobbed
helplessly into my hands. Nevertheless, even now—
despite every betrayal, all those botched dreams:
the woman I could not forgive, the children
who never came back, myself the same fool, only
grayer & stooped; even now, understanding at last
that there's no disembarking, no turning back,
that the world itself is nothing but motion:
ephemeral, flickering, emptiness whirling in space—
there are times when I still refuse to believe it, times
when the wretched deceit of it all overcomes me,
& suddenly I'll leap to my feet—yes,
even now—with the old indignation & terror.
"Now see here," I cry out. "Now see here!"

To Tell the Literal Truth

is the trick by which poetry, Rico was saying, anchors itself
to the actual world (I had been rash enough to suggest
that in art the literal truth doesn't matter a bit),
when a coiled rattler, a good four feet of her, stretched
in the heat on the ill-marked Moorfred Rivercrest
trail we'd been hiking, startled us out of our chatter.
We didn't breathe, gave her a wide berth, & were safely past,
when Zoly, our Aussie companion, who'd just gotten back
from a month-long dig in the outback pits of Rodinga
—Zoly, who cares not a whit for epistemological theory—
did something I'll never forget: in one swift motion swiveled,
bent, & grabbed for her throat, the other hand closing
above that whiplash of rattles, then, with a grin, rose to his feet.
The creature writhed in his hands, buzzed with her hideous
rattles while she hissed with her godawful tongues
& tried to break free. Rico & me, we jumped back in terror.
Zoly, holding her out for us to admire, said "*Crotalus atrox*:
Western Diamondback. Marvelous specimen, no?"
I could care less what it was called. I took another step back.
Zoly strode to an outcrop of boulders a few yards away,
& gently as setting a kid in its crib, & with only the tiniest
flourish—the sort a jaunty conductor or close-up
magician might make—tossed the thing free.
It vanished, instantaneously, slithering into the rocks.
I took a deep breath & relaxed. From where we stood,
on that rise, you could make out the Salton Sea, far
to the east, & the undulant floor of the desert a long drop below,
endless & dreamlike. "Amazing!" Rico mumbled
under his breath, lifting his Padres cap & rubbing the sweat
from his brow. But whether he meant the vista, or snake,
or how quickly it vanished, or what Zoly had done,
or the whole delectable drift of the thing, god only knows.
Listen: In art, the truth—in that sense—doesn't matter.

I made the whole story up. The Aussie. The outback.
The snake. Even the name of the trail. All but the part
where two friends & I argue over the poet's
relationship to the literal fact. Everything else in this poem is a lie.

Personality Parade

After Watergate, wasn't Richard Nixon secretly committed to a
mental institution run by Quakers and replaced by the CIA with
a Hollywood double? Isn't this the real reason why his wife, Pat,
refuses all interviews because she is afraid reporters will ask about
the look-alike she is living with, and she will have to tell?
                                    M. P., New Brighton, Minn.
                              ("Walter Scott's Personality Parade")

When they carted Dick off that morning,
Pat was frankly upset. It wasn't just
that they'd caught him making his
I-am-innocent speech out on Park Avenue,
naked except for his black inaugural tie,
or because of the screams of that little girl
they'd found in the basement, tied to a drainpipe—
after all, Dick had done crazier things in the White House.
But it was dread of another scandal,
one more call from the *Washington Post*,
another smug chuckle from Walter Cronkite.
She was sick & tired of wearing dark glasses,
a fake rubber nose & a thick mustache in public.
So when Central Intelligence mentioned
a permanent rest-home for Dick in Tierra del Fuego,
Pat jumped at the chance, though at first
when the Hollywood double showed up at the door
she'd had her misgivings. A failed vaudevillian,
he could never pass thru the dining salon
without leaping up on the table
for one final chorus of *Sweet Georgia Brown*,
his glazed eyes rolling like Eddie Cantor.
He'd softshoe his way thru their afternoon strolls,
break into Gene Kelly routines when no one
was looking, tell unfunny jokes from the '30s.

[19]

His squirt-in-the-eye boutonniere never amused her.
He reeked of a dozen colognes.
It was only at night, on the springs,
that she had to admit that his flashy showbiz routines
were a hundred percent more entertaining
than Dick ever was with his shrill little whines
& pasty caresses & minuscule twanger.
When she thought of the old days
she'd let out a heartrending sigh—of relief,
& bending down as he jawed on the phone with his agent
or checked thru the casting calls in the latest issue
of *Billboard,* she'd offer her sweet little hoofer a peck
on the cheek—at which he would drop whatever it was
he'd been doing, & grinning, give a little flick of his head
so the bowler he wore indoors & out would slide down
his arm in a deft double-gainer & land at his fingers—
Pat's cue to two-step around him, & taking his arm
they would *pas-de-deux* into the bedroom,
popping their heads out once thru the doorway
by way of finale, the whole number accomplished,
if you can believe it, while belting out a novelty
two-part arrangement of *Blue Skies* . . .
nothing but blue skies from now on.

Memorial Day

Because our sons adore their plastic missile launchers,
electronic space bazookas, neutron death-ray guns,
a decade down the pike it won't prove difficult
to trick them out in combat boots
& camouflage fatigues,
rouse them with a frenzy of parades, the heady
rhetoric of country, camaraderie & God,
the drum & bugle & the sudden
thunder of the cannon as they march
into Hell singing.
Which is the order of things.
Obedient to a fault, the people will do as they are told.
However dispirited by grief at the graves
of their fallen, the mother returns at last to her loom,
the father to his lathe,
& the inconsolable widow home to raise sons
ardent for the next imperial bloodbath:
    Ilium. Thermopylae. Verdun. Pork Chop Hill.

Will Boland & I

stroll from Dog Beach down to Cape May, grumbling
over this nation's inexhaustible
predilection for carnage: the mask of rectitude
painted over the skull of vindictive rage.
It is midwinter, the beach all but deserted:
an elderly gent walks an elderly golden retriever;
a family of four is out hunting for shells;
two good old boys chugging their Michelobs
take in the last of the sunset:
down at their feet, Iwo Jimaed into the sand,
a colossal American flag
that they've lugged down here to the beach
with their cooler of beer to cheer on the home team.
Night & day, on the other side of the world,
daisy-cutters are pounding a village
to shambles, bathing the landscape in blood.
Women crouch in the rubble rocking their dead.
         —*Listen*, I say to Will.
E. O. Wilson can swear up & down there are species
of ants even more compulsively homicidal
than man: I, for one, remain unconvinced.

Above us, that gorgeous midwinter dusk.
At our feet, the Pacific, ablaze in magentas & red.
True enough, he ventures, *but Steve, you've got*
to admit we're just as much a part of this world
as anything else . . . & maybe,
in some crazy way, marvelous too!
         I shrug.
We walk on in silence.
A couple of high school girls,
frolicking in & out of the surf, smile up at us sweetly.
    A part of this world, yes, I snarl back.

But surely the ugliest part!—the words hardly
out of my mouth when those two young women,
now twenty yards or so down the beach,
suddenly fling open their arms, rise to their toes,
leap into the air, & float there—angelic . . . unearthly . . .
impossibly luminous creatures, alighting
at last in a dazzle of pirouettes & glissades,
only to rise up into the air again & again, while Will
& I stand there—dumbfounded, grinning, amazed.
Under the flare of the night's first stars
each *grande jeté* more splendid, rapturous,
vaulting! Two ardently schooled young ballerinas,
silhouetted against the indigo flames
of the darkening western horizon.
The last of the light of this world setting behind them.

Invocation to My Muses

Never having had a muse to call my own, I bought one of those dollar-
ninety-eight cent novelty ballpoint pens in San Francisco
with a pair of winsome if diminutive young bathing beauties
in the barrel's laminated plastic window & adopted them.
Now when I spew forth my homicidal odes against the Pax Americana,
maledictions at the banks & the shenanigans of finance capital,
philippics on the snuffing of entire populations, strophes full
of *weltschmerz* & angst, my lilliputian muses in their little string
bikinis are a constant source of solace & of inspiration.
& when I pen paeonics to the Absolute, that ballpoint bounding
like some Chassid master or Mavlavi dervish dancing on the rooftops
in a rapture of transcendent union, my two voluptuary muses
romp among the dunes of every cursive.
Wallow as I will in the most metaphysical & speculative slough:
my choriambics on the noumenal & the mysterion, hendecasyllables
upon continual creation, Anselm's Argument, & Rodney Collin's
catalogue of the invisible, they hang on every word:
they do not flit about from bard to bard & bed to bed like fickler muses
but are ever modest, steadfast, chaste & loyal.
Whatever be my measure or my mode: be I apostrophizing,
rhapsodizing, waxing lyrical or wringing dry the tissue of the heart,
or simply sketching dithyrambic jubilees to the quotidian, poetry
in praise of almost anything, my fetching midinettes remain
as decorous as Lady Astor, steadfast as Penelope, as faithful
& as innocent as honest labor, fuzzy mittens, chamomile tea. . . .
Or so indeed they seem when that sleek pen figure-eights
along the page. But—O wretched moment—when the inspiration flags
& my elbow leans against the armrest so that the upturned point
faces skyward like a suppliant toward Paradise,
& my mini-terpsichoreans, perforce upended, end up standing
on their heads like fallen women, then—O things grow sticky!
For obedient in that posture to some cosmic law known
only to our Beloved Maker, those teeny sky-blue two-piece swimsuits
clinging to their saucy torsos begin unaccountably dissolving!

It's miraculous! Astonishing! Unnerving! My muses start a slow,
seductive, disconcerting & mysterious disrobing!—
some newfangled kind of gravity-induced striptease that renders them
as naked as a pair of peeled tomatoes, nude as two unfigleaved Eves,
or as Susanna ogled in her garden by licentious Elders,
or as Artemis the day Actaeon went to pieces having seen her
in the altogether, bathing—irresistibly, lubriciously, shamelessly
& absolutely naked from their silky golden tresses
to their teeny rosy toenails! O my own sweet Thalia & Erato!
Dear uninhibited half-sisters, nude from those erectile
areolas to those pert, alluring mini-*montes veneris*.
O music never to be finished! *Poetastus interruptus!*
Jettisoned Porlockian epiphanies adrift upon the Lethean & swift
amnesiatic waters of the void! & yet, withal, blithe spirits,
I do swear, despite the fact that my interminable apostrophes
upon your nubile, sweet & lickerish anatomies continually distract me
from completing my sublime librettos to the Infinite, my Orphic hymns
to the Millennium, & even if it comes to that, forever blows my chance
to cop a Prix de Rome, MacArthur, Pulitzer, or Guggenheim,
I will—I swear—prove equal to your rapturous burlesque.
I shall rise to the occasion & will not forsake you, ever! But prove worthy
of those much maligned though everywhere obliquely honored,
warm, priapic, & exalted pleasures of the flesh! O lasciviest of muses,
for your own parts, when I roll your tiny midriffs through my fingers
like a stricken, inarticulate King Kong, facing for your lusty sakes
the murderous concerted armies of the critics—prove ye
likewise faithful! May your sizzling, uninhibited striptease inspire verse
forever fecund, vibrant, earthy, gracious, steadfast, wise & strong!
Sweet dames, runne softly till I end my song.

For Chile

In the offices
of Anaconda-
Kennecott
cigar ash
drops
into an ashtray
like a severed head.

In the streets
of Santiago
the long struggle
of Lautaro
& Manuel Rodriguez
goes on,
as the heaviness
of a man's heart
becomes the heaviness
of his fist.

Golden Delicious

When old Frieda Holden, the lady from whom
I would buy those wonderful apples, started raving
about the new young pastor
at First Church of Christ, Savior,
on Lansing & Mission,
I thought Jesus, I'm in for it now,
& tuned out—that is to say,
as I stood in the doorway
watching her bag two dozen Golden Delicious
out of a barrel-sized crate,
I nodded & grinned.
"Well, that's awfully nice . . . " I would mumble.
You know how it goes—that catechism
of slavish politeness. Like one of those shriveled
colonial apple-head dolls, the old lady
was nothing but wrinkles,
with blotched, cadaverous arms,
& hands that would never stop shaking.
Wasted away like she was she was scary
to look at. Now I've never liked Jesus talk much:
it jangles my nerves.
Nor do I have any great love for that merciless,
apoplectic Old Testament God—
a paranoid schizoaffective
fixated on vengeance. *No, frankly,*
I haven't the least bit of interest in either
your church or its priesthood,
is what I was seething to tell her.
Not, I suppose, as I'd like to believe,
from some urge to correct her view of the world
or deepen the level of discourse between us.
But simply to rag her . . .
that old instinct of mine

for schoolboy defiance: a braggart's need
to assert that I'd thought about things
more deeply than she had, was worldly
in ways that she wasn't, moved
in a universe larger by far
than that circumscribed province of fruit trees
& churches & country politeness.

                              "Compassion,"
she said out of nowhere—or rather,
half whispered.
"Isn't that now the root from which spirit springs? . . . "
& handing over the bag
with the two dozen apples,
she looked at me sweetly.
                       Had I been dreaming?
I stood there a moment embarrassed, fumbling
for change, then thanked her profusely
& stumbled back to my Datsun.

Halfway home, one hand on the wheel,
the other holding one of those juicy Golden
Deliciouses up to my mouth,
it hit me. Of course.
It wasn't an admonition brought on by something
she'd seen, in some creepy way, in my soul,
but merely a phrase that her minister used
that had stuck, & that she was repeating to me
in a context I'd missed.
And once that was clear,
the hard pit of breath caught in my chest released
itself from my throat, half
sigh & half laugh. In truth, nothing at all
had in fact passed between us but neighborly tidings,

the old convivial graces.
She'd simply been trying to give me some sense
of the man she so much admired,
& of the faith they belonged to,
& of who she herself was—the adamant spirit
under that crumbling flesh.
For all of my rage at her church, not a cell of me
wished the old woman less than good health & long life.
Or, since long life she had in abundance,
if there was anything to it, life everlasting.

& that settled between myself & my demons,
I took one more bite of that wonderful apple
& rose back into this vivid world.
In the last flush of daylight the roofs
of occasional houses & barns
caught the crimson of sunset. Horses & cows
stood about in their perfect stillness.
Behind them, this world, growing darker
—all ruddy & golden—had started dissolving.

                    Compassion—
isn't that now the root from which spirit springs
rolled around on my tongue
with its fine, sweet taste, till that too
vanished into the hum
of the tires spinning over that backcountry road
like some kind of music.

That Ecstasy of Kisses

3 a.m.

in the Florida night
& the neighbor's daughter
steps out of a Chevy
& stands
on the pavement
leaning her weight on one hip,
adjusting her halter
& cut-offs,
& combing her hair in the moonlight,
a shower of scarlet,
the blooms
of the poinciana,
falling about her.

For My Neighbor's Daughter

Afraid that your eyes will smart
painfully in the summer's glare,
you seldom go out anymore
without those dark glasses.
Nor do you wear those fetching
summer dresses,
the ones that spin about
as you swirl down the street.
Is it because of this insufferable heat
that you have begun neglecting
your wardrobe & makeup
& letting your long hair spill uncombed
down your back—this heat,
which has turned everything too bright,
too melancholic?
It is easier, I know, to find delicate
crystal that will not break
than a boy who means what he says.
Still, that is no reason
to sit in the dark
of your mother's porch,
night after hot August night,
with only the light of that small radio
glowing beside you.
Given a town filled with young men
who love dancing & fast cars,
do not, sweet child,
redden your eyes all summer long
for a boy who is not coming back.

Youngstown

Sweet now to recall that August noon
pushed decades back
into the soft machine.
The peace that someone's old Ford
left us with,
& late that night
the cabin
out of Youngstown
where we lay in darkness
& each other's arms,
the night deserted
but for the bereaving cries
the crickets cried
out in the woods somewhere,
& up in arms
at every single kiss,
buzzing like gossips
at the windowscreens,
the moral indignation of the flies.
You'd think they'd never seen
such goings-on as this.

Days of '65

I want it back—that sixth floor walk-up
with its lilac curtains. City
full of sirens, bookshops, dim cafes.

I want the candles & the rum,
the fevered talk. A flickering of neon
thru the blinds. That bong's sweet scent

& glow. Che's photo taped above
my ancient stereo. Some angel
purring softly in the dark. A plaintive
keyboard . . . sultry horn . . . insistent drum.

Sweater

Evening. That tiny place in Detroit.
Mother sits in her frayed
housedress, knitting & dozing.
Your father, Odysseus—God knows
where he is—left decades ago.
Unlike the famous story,
the sweater your mom knits
is intact. It is for you.
At night, alone, her life slowly unravels.

The Girls of Malibu

From the California beach town where I live, I drove
to Lindbergh Field, then caught a flight to Vegas
& drove grimly up the strip to my hotel. I loathe the place:
what Himalayas are to heights, Las Vegas is to Hell.

But money's tight & if they offer me the job I guess I—
well, we'll see. Too early yet to crash, I punch
the TV on & spin the knob. The usual late-night trash:
league bowling, MTV, a talk-show interview as puerile

as the late night movie—till I flip to something kitschy
& X-rated: the Girls of Malibu talk breathlessly
about their lives, then strip & writhe about & stroke
their breasts to look the way one looks when getting laid.

Exploitative & sexist? But of course. Nonetheless,
I think them nicely made. One lisps. Another coos
how much she really loves to whore.
They talk about their lives & bare their loins.

One's lost an only brother in the war.
One's folks back in Des Moines have no idea
she plies the trade she does. There's something touching
in the way they talk, even if their stories are all lies,

a kind of cinema verité effect that's more revealing
than their predictable stripteases.
It makes them less lascivious but more appealing.
I hang my only suit up thinking, Jesus, would I really

cash the life I have been loving in for gold?
Shaking open at her waist a velvet sash,
Joella slips out of her camisole, delicious whitecaps
breaking on the beach behind her. California:

that hazy red Pacific sunset that can take your breath.
"I swear—I'd do, I mean, well, almost anything,"
confesses Tracy Sue, for both of us,
"to—well, you know, like . . . get to stay out here."

Eurydice

Everything you've heard about that irresistibly seductive
lyre of his is true. And yes, the birds would light
upon the overhanging branches & grow still
to hear him pluck its strings. No creature who had ears
could not be moved—nor was it music
only, but himself, that he was sweet & passionate
& innocent, that won me to him. As with everything
about that boy, his love was absolute. Exquisite
music not because his hands were lithe,
but that his spirit sang—though truth to tell
he was in many ways a child: impetuous, unthinking,
willful in the way a child is, who in his single-mindedness
& the immensity of his desire
cares nothing that the matter is impossible.
Am I to blame him for that one mistake?
Is one to blame the child who overturns the lamp & sets
the house aflame? No, no! He loved me. I will not betray—
It was his nature—foolish . . . well, perhaps, but
how cast blame? Who else, inflamed by such
enraptured grief, would have stormed Hell
to lead me back into that sun-drenched earth?
We climbed through this abysmal dark for days,
myself so close behind I could have stretched my hand
& touched his shoulder blade, if touching were a thing
the dead could do.—Oh, who would be so cruel
that she would blame that boy whose only crime
was childish impatience & impulsive love—whose only
sin was that he longed for me so fervently
that when he saw at last the rosy light of that
bright world above the hills that marks the cusp of Earth
he was so overcome with joy that he . . . I mean . . . No!
I dare not speak of it—that brainless, stupefying
fatal final glance that whirled me back into this bitter dark.

Endymion

Because of his inhuman beauty,
Selene, goddess of the moon,
embraced him
with her fatal love.
So the young shepherd, Endymion,
lies there on the Latmian hillside
wrapped in a sleep
from which he will not waken.
Beside him graze the innocent sheep.
In the moonlight, everything silver,
everything perfectly still.

Batik

Above our bed
beside the amber light,
a jeweled
hermaphroditic Krshna
from Nepal
with scarlet lips,
elongated white eyes—
the god
love-struck
& sensuous
& melancholic.

Flying

*Seven former followers of bearded guru Maharishi Mahesh Yogi
have gone to court claiming the famed mystic is a failure—because
he didn't teach them to fly. . . . "Flying constituted hopping with
the legs folded in the lotus position," said the guru's grounded ex-
disciples. . . . Each wants $9 million from the Maharishi.*

                                                   Weekly World News

What we did, Your Honor,
was hop up & down on the floor
with our legs pretzeled together,
when what I had paid for
was for my parents to see me
sail gracefully over the rooftops
so I could wave down,
kicking a little for speed,
like I was swimming.
"That's my kid up there!" my old man
would say to the neighbors
as if it were nothing, but all
afternoon he'd stand there
pretending to water the lawn, looking
over his shoulder & grinning.
Instead, Your Honor, the *kundalini*
the Maharishi said
was going to waken & rise
from inside my ethereal body
& set me aloft turned out
to be less a coiled serpent
asleep at the base of my spine
than a kind of horrible
bedspring stuck to the seat
of my pants & on which
—to my mom's utter chagrin

[43]

& my dad's shocked disgust,
& the unending jibes of all
my kid sister's circle of friends,
for whom I was simply
Herman the Yo-yo,
the world's most kickable clown—
I'd bounce up & down,
night & day, reciting my mantra,
eyes floating in tears,
praying at every moment
to rise off that carpet & sail
thru that window & out of that
house once & for all—
to disappear over the suburbs,
into the clouds, like a bird
that had broken out of his cage,
or the fragile balloon of a child
that someone who hadn't
been careful enough had let go of.

A True History of Good King Clodysus

for Minas Savvas

After that pernicious tyrant died, the crown was both by right
& acclamation passed to good Clodysus, his beloved brother.
At once, the former monarch's son assailed the court
with wild accusations that his mother & usurping uncle
had colluded in his father's murder. Evidence? His sire's ghost,
stalking at night about the parapets, had told him so!
Patently unbalanced & already famously delusional,
the nervous nephew cackled his demented slanders while
the subjects of that kingdom shook their heads & bit their tongues.

But when the counselors to the throne insisted that the prince,
incurably deranged, must not be suffered to remain alive,
lest those malignant fables undermine the tranquil virtues
of his reign, that gentle king (who if possessed of any flaw,
it was a heart too willing to forgive) commanded that his troubled
nephew be, instead, escorted to some peaceful hamlet
on the outskirts of the realm, there to humor his dark fancies
free from harm: a plan, alas, that horribly miscarried,
for the lunatic struck down a pair of trusted friends,
an aged minister of state, the old man's maiden daughter
(whom he drowned), then set a cup of poisoned mead
beside his mother's plate & seeing her drop smartly
to the ground set fire to the king's bedchamber,
chortling merrily to watch Clodysus screaming in the flames.

O never did a kingdom grieve as Denmark grieved!
The wretch was apprehended, tried & hung, though not
before the kingdom had been wracked by blood & torn apart
by chaos & dissension. Although accurate accounts
of those events were dutifully recorded by the scribes & court
historians, down the centuries the annals for the year 917

have disappeared, & nothing of that record now remains
but versions so corrupted that ethnographers are still at pains
to sift the facts from a millennial accretion of elaborate lies.

One version, done up for the stage by some befuddled hack
has the entire business backwards—villains, heroes,
every circumstance confused. That bedlamite, with all
his florid, broody, overwrought soliloquizing, storms
around the stage, the very figure of conflicted grace:
an imbecilic farce invented for a savage & untutored age,
yet one that to this very day, for all its bluster, flummery & bathos,
has been periodically exhumed by stage-struck neophytes
at amateur theatricals & dreary little dinner theaters in the provinces.

The Grammar Lesson

for Dorianne

A noun's a thing. A verb's the thing it does.
An adjective is what describes the noun.
In "The can of beets is filled with purple fuzz,"

of and *with* are prepositions. *The's*
an article, a *can's* a noun.
A noun's a thing. A verb's the thing it does.

A can *can* roll—or not. What isn't was
or might be, *might* meaning not yet known.
"Our can of beets *is* filled with purple fuzz"

is present tense. While words like *our* and *us*
are pronouns—i.e., *it* is moldy, *they* are icky brown.
A noun's a thing; a verb's the thing it does.

Is is a helping verb. It helps because
filled isn't a full verb. *Can's* what *our* owns
in "*Our* can of beets is filled with purple fuzz."

See? There's nothing to it. Just
memorize these simple rules . . . or write them down:
a noun's a thing; a verb's the thing it does.
The can of beets is filled with purple fuzz.

Poor Bishop Berkeley

exists only when I think about him,
& I haven't thought about him in years.

Brief Note to Varus

Varus, have you heard the news?
Our friend Suffenus, arch-sophisticate & wit,
has, sad to say, gone daft
& can't stop shoveling a manuscript
of the most sophomoric verse
in everybody's face, the sort
of jejune treacle lovesick adolescents
love to write, & worse, fancies half the presses
in the nation vying for the privilege
of publishing that mawkish tripe.
It's gotten so on seeing him we duck,
terrified he'll noodle more of that
unstomachable slop our way. How quick
his tongue once was to lash out at the sham,
bombastic & grandiloquent, who nowadays
pens nothing but—imagining, with not a drop
of shame, that he's a shoe-in for a Lannan
Prize, MacArthur, & a Prix de Rome.
This recitation of Suffenus's obsession
being sketched for you, dear Varus,
not at all to vilify our noble, formerly swift-
witted friend (who, any luck, will be his old
self soon again), but on yourself to urge this caveat:
of all sins to be wary of, beware self-praise.
It is impossible to see the pimple on one's own chin.
                    Ever your faithful servant,
                        Gaius Valerius Catullus

Vivamus . . .

Come, my Lesbia, let us live & love.
Why fret that covetous old men
find for their tongues no fitter use
than gossip? What of it?
Let them reap their nickel's worth of fun.
Unerringly, at every dawn, the sun
arises from its dark, forsaken sleep.
Love, not so with us: the light,
when once extinguished from these eyes,
begets a night from which we shall not wake.
Kiss me a hundred thousand times
& then ten thousand times ten hundred
thousand more. Confounded thus,
their babble will be hushed
by our unutterable bliss:
this rapture that will strike all envy dumb,
this ecstasy of kisses without number.

Catullus: Carmina 5

Interstate 69: A Preliminary Report

I regret to say that we of the FBI are powerless to act in cases of oral-genital intimacy, unless it has in some way obstructed interstate commerce.

J. Edgar Hoover

For months now, thousands of 18-wheelers have been pulling
off onto the gravel embankments & soft shoulders.
Their engines purr a moment or two & grow still.
From darkened cabs comes that mysterious, horrible moaning.
Crates of bananas grow soft in the trailers.
Maggots crawl through potatoes;
a white slime oozes over the plums.
Trucks full of lug nuts & pistons & nylons & blenders
fail to show up at the loading dock, the company warehouse.
Only the devil knows what sorts of unnatural acts
have been going down out there on that long truckers' haul
between East Saginaw & Fort Wayne,
that six-lane interstate crossing the Indiana-Michigan line.
But one thing's for damn sure—these days nothing
in cherry condition or edible ever gets through.
& whatever the reason, the thing is clearly
too big for the state boys to handle:
If ever a case cried out for the Feds, this one is it!

Theology

That Salome,
she sure could dance.

Bumstead

Though he tremble in front of the boss,
at home he defends the idea
of the 4-day work week
with eloquent logic:
as swiftly it slips from his tongue
as leaves fall
from the book of days.
In the final frame,
Dagwood the uncomplaining,
that latter-day saint
of domestic virtue,
who finds himself middle-aged
& increasingly desperate for time,
stands in front of his mirror
reflecting his fate
& rehearsing how he will put it
to Mr. Dithers,
which is,
for him, I assure you, sweet reader,
no laughing matter.

That Other Life

Tungurahua

& one afternoon Verne & I trekked thru the hills
toward that cone of mauve light
that we spotted at last
looming over the eastern horizon, its peak
miles above us, mantled in snow—the Andes
immense, exquisite, rolling away in every direction.
We sat down to watch it & rest,
the sun behind us,
the world aglow in its ruddy blush.
I pulled a handful of *hojas* out of my pouch
& broke a black wafer of lime into bits,
as the Quechua people have done for hundreds of years,
& rolled us a couple of hits.
We sat there a long while in silence,
rising at last to begin the long haul back to Baños
thru the Andean dusk,
hiking thru fields of tiny & luminous flowers:
salmon & blue & vermilion.
Me & Verne Schultz,
there in that other life, decades ago.
The dark, bitter juices dripping into our throats.
Hojas de coca: vice of the old Incas themselves.

Southern Atlantic

"Didn't touch a drink
for sixteen years,
but when the wife died . . . "
The 5 a.m. drizzle
had brought him out
of the high weeds
by the railroad tracks
where he slept,
to find shelter
under the tin roof
of the warehouse
I was night watchman of.
He loaded crates
when he needed,
he said, or picked fruit
in the fields. "But mostly
nothing . . . mostly I just
pass the days. . . . Jeanette,"
I remember him saying.
"Jeanette with two t's . . . .
That's what now . . . eight,
ten years . . . ?"
Then, when the rain let up,
with a little hobo salute,
he turned & was gone.
From the loading dock
of Southern Atlantic
Fruit, you could see
tugs on the river,
& out past the turnpike
& palms, the skyline
of downtown Miami,
all cream & pastel.
& beyond, out on the bay,

south of the city,
that long white causeway
heading into the Keys.

The Bridge

Climbed up past the ridge,
slipped off my pack,
& sat there
on that viewy overhang,
the emerald vista
vast & luminous
as I'd remembered.
A pair of hawks
circled slowly far below.
The world is opulent,
indifferent, undeceitful.
Still & all, its latter purposes
elude us.
Brushing away a fly
that had been buzzing
at my skull,
I dug out of my pack
a pippin apple.
At my feet, flakes of mica
glistened
in the faceted conglomerate,
& to my left, suspended
from two stalks
of mountain lilac
past their bloom,
a miniature bridge:
the swaying membrane
of a web
some solitary spider
had abandoned—
a single strand,
half glowing in the light,
& half invisible.

Night Falls in the Lagunas

Sliver of lightning like a hairline
fracture, but no rain.
I hike back to my tent alone
—distraught, disquieted.
Stellar's Jays
squawking in the Jeffrey pines
thru which a bone white
moon is rising. Suddenly
the frenzied yapping of coyotes
in the dark: they too,
unreconciled to this world.
Coyotes, crying out
to one another from all sides.

Passing Thru

Astonishing, isn't it—all of these odd-
looking creatures darting around
in the grass—the lizards
& spiders & foraging bugs,
& the ones that are nothing but dots
of color flitting around
on invisible wings,
each with its own private sorrows
& pleasures,
its one precious life.
How strange it is
to be here at all
talking to you like this
in a poem,
if just for a single brief instant—
two spirits momentarily touching.
Isn't it weird?
Don't you feel it too,
how unspeakably odd everything is?
Friend, walk mindfully here:
Do no intentional harm.
Even the least of these creatures,
the tiniest sentient speck,
longs to live out
its one brief season on Earth.

Translator's Note

Friend, if these verses
seem inconsequential
& clumsy,
a macaronic concoction
of tortured devices,
metrical gaffes,
& bloated conceits,
incapable
for so much as a single
figure or phrase
of wrenching the spirit
awake
to the rapture
& grief of this world,
please keep in mind
that what you've been reading
are nothing
but quickly assembled
slipshod translations.
O patient,
long-suffering reader,
I swear it
upon all I hold sacred:
In the original tongue
these poems
are absolutely sublime.

Wreath

An oval of paper flowers
nailed to a post
on the shoulder of I-94
near the Mexican border.
Daisies & mums
framing a snapshot:
the guy who got killed
right there on that spot.
Someone who stares out
every night at the dark
when no one's around
nailed it up out here
in the middle of nowhere.
It flashes in and out
of your sight
as you drive through
these high desert hills.
For the briefest of moments
everything is what it is,
blindingly real.
But for only that moment.
Then everything's back
as it was. After all,
you've got places to get to.
Plans. Obligations.
A million things on your mind.

Denis, Some Photos

It's not the one of you on the steps with Andy & Robert & Phil,
the four of you mugging with macho cigars: four tough union scrappers,
or the one in the corduroy jacket & dark biker shades,
or the broodingly handsome young stud in the wool sweater,
scraggly of beard, your rock-star hair gorgeously long.
God knows who snapped that one more than a decade ago.
Or the one at the table, amused & relaxed next to Alma, who's beaming.
Not even that juicy portrait of you in your leather jacket & baseball cap
standing next to Norma Hernandez, looking so much yourself, so fully
alive that it's scary, so beguiling & scruffy, so filled with that vivid,
dashing, mischievous air you had always about you. Denis,
you're so close in that photo I think I could take one little step forward
& hug you again. But not even that one. The one that I'm talking about
is you by yourself in the desert, at sunset, in shadow. Maybe
it's east of Santee or out in the Anza-Borrego. You in your jacket & jeans,
right arm extended behind you, palm open, gesturing back
toward those incandescent mauve hills, the sky a luminous blue
brushed with the purples of dusk; in the uppermost left a white cloud
fringed in sandía red like some kind of halo: mysterious, ethereal. You
in the quiet dark with that puckish grin: half Irish wit & half tender grace,
pleased with it all. The sweep of your arm as much as to say *Look!*
This is just what I meant. What I've been trying to say the whole time!
See, it's exactly this I've been wanting to tell you. & after it's snapped,
I can just hear that wry, ironic grunt of your satisfied, shy
metaphysical laugh. The one of you by yourself, in a gesture
of absolute welcome, under a sky glowing at sunset, behind you those hills
& that white oracular cloud far to the left with its rapturous halo, portent
of all things that cannot be spoken. & you, ever the sweet host. *C'mon,*
you're saying. *Let's keep on walking. We'll get even closer.* It's that one.

Denis Callahan, 1957-2006

Raven

Squawks from a raven in what used to be Jack
Funk's field over the fence, scolding me
till I look up & see that the hills
are still there, that the day
couldn't be lovelier, sweeter. Susan Greene's
little girls are chatting in singsong
up in the treehouse
in what used to be Dempsey's old place
to the west. Mary, who will stroll over these four-
point-five acres of rolling high desert chaparral
when we two are gone?—The tin barn,
the pumphouse & shed. That underground
stream from which we've been drinking
our fill these fifteen years.
Who'll own all this dusty blue mountain lilac,
the aloe & roses & pines & bright orange iceplant?
Who'll walk in the shade of that live oak
under which Ralphie & Ivan & Charlie,
& Eddie are buried? Who'll watch the quail
flutter out of the brush in formation
& the rabbits scurry for cover? Who
will these granite boulders & lovely agaves
belong to when you & I, beloved, are buried
& long forgotten?—Forgive me,
sweet earth, for not being shaken more often
out of the heavy sleep of the self. *Wake up!*
Wake up! scolds the raven, sailing off
over the canyon. *Wake up! Wake up! Wake up!*

Rest Stop

To piss, I pull into the rest stop off Interstate 10, halfway
between Tucson & Casa Grande. It's three in the morning.
The scented sage desert so delectably hot
I could weep. Then too, there's that full orange moon,
almost too big to be true. Man's fate, when all's said & done,
isn't the issue. On the wall above the urinal someone
has written LIBERATE JESUS. Liberate Jesus? Outside,
a fellow who's fallen asleep in the bed of his pickup
is happily snoring. Three young dudes hunker
by the stone fountain smoking & shooting the bull.
An elderly woman leans on her walker
sucking the juice from a pear. Behind
her, a handful of unlit Rec V's. Then nothing but desert.
Palo verdes & yucca. Not a single subdivision or mall.
After we're gone—not just this infinitely sanctimonious nation-
state, but the whole duplicitous, bloodthirsty human crew—
it will still be here. Well pleased, I slide behind the wheel
of my little yellow Tercel & cruise back onto 10 West.
The woman with her walker, the guy catching some Z's,
the friends hunkering there in the night, smoking
& chatting, I wish them all well. I slip in another CD:
Hollow Bamboo. Figure to make Yuma by dawn.
I think of that God of Love flinging millions of souls
into Hell, of the puffed-up, fantastic beliefs
of this tiny featherless biped. That aside,
the night about as fragrant & paradisiacal as it gets.
Spectacular moon low in the west. Ry Cooder's
guitar. Ronu Majumdar's bamboo flute. Desert on both sides.

After Surgery

I hobble up the driveway holding Mary's arm & leaning
on that old collapsible black cane
that years ago I thought I'd put away for good.
A week ago this life was nothing but intolerable pain,
but now it's rather wonderful again.
Raymond, goofily delighted that we're strolling
thru the dark, lopes on ahead: *Make way! Make way!*
he barks delightedly. An all but moonless night
in which we have stepped out to look at Mars,
just past the driveway, over the Tecate hills, huge
& glowing in the eastern sky & closer to the Earth
than it has been in slightly under sixty thousand years.
—*No*, Mary shakes her head, *that can't be Mars.*
That thing's too bright . . . too big. Peering at it
through those old binoculars, she tells me that she's certain
what it is I've been admiring up there is just
another border patrol chopper hovering above
the canyons between here & Mexico, chasing down
some band of hapless *campesinos* working
their way north.—*No, it's Mars alright! I'd recognize it*
anywhere! I say authoritatively, as is my wont.
& pointing with that hollow cane of mine
to where it gleams—as bold & asymmetrical
as any of those feverish-looking asterisks I scribble
in the margins of my books, marking passages
that seem absolutely right or marvelously put, & worth
(O sweet & foolish dream) returning to some day
when I have time—I patiently explain to her that Mars
is just where it's supposed to be: straight up
the driveway, past Coyote Holler Road, where we
ourselves are standing, looking east. Gleeful, tail awag,
Ray hunkers down & looks east too, expectantly,
while I, inspired at last, & flourishing that hollow wand

of mine, as Johannes Kepler might himself have,
centuries ago—trace, among that intricate vast circuitry
of stars, the constellation of Krokidium (the Bloated Frog)
& Balthor & Valdubius—exactly where they'd have
no choice but find themselves this time of night
above the planet Earth, there in the August sky.
Mary, dutifully impressed, takes my arm
& heads us back, suggesting that for all we know
there's not a single one of all those stars that even
has existed for a million years. *Ridiculous!* I bellow.
*If they didn't exist just how the hell could we be looking
up at them?!* To which she mumbles something
that I won't repeat, & kisses me, & slips her arm
around my waist & says it's nice to have me home.
I wince, & hobble eight or ten more feet, & look up
at the sky for one last time, & tell her just what any
self-respecting star might well have said if it could speak:
Honey, you can't believe how glad I am I still exist.

Kelly Park

Late fall. Gray macadam Brooklyn afternoon.
The Brighton local rumbles on its trestle
over Kelly Park. We're pedaling 3-speed bikes
around the baseball field, the big kids
belting fungoes toward the fence.
This bike of mine, it never had a right-hand
rubber grip. It's blue & yellow
with a rusted bell. How cold
that handlebar still is against my palm!
Right here I lean into that frigid gust. Then
turn, the wind at last behind me. Look!
This is the moment when I pick up speed.
At the crack of the bat, the ball at once
both rises toward the left field fence
& drops into a fielder's waiting glove—
all this in one swift parabolic arc. Who
could have guessed it would rush by so fast?
November. Brooklyn. 1950-something. Kelly Park.

Song

Up half the night
fitfully tossing.
A cock crows,
& another
further away.
A dim,
distant star
flickers
& disappears
like human ambition.
We too
flapped our wings,
sang our brief song,
& were gone.

Acknowledgments

I am grateful to the editors of the following journals and other publications in which some of the poems in this book first appeared: *Chiron Review, CityBender, Caprice, The California Review, Friction, Mangrove, Margie, Triplopia,* and *The Sun.* Some poems originally appeared in the following anthologies and books: *An Eye for An Eye Makes the Whole World Blind: Poets on 9/11,* Allen Cohen and Clive Matson, eds. (Regent Press, 2002); *In the Palm of Your Hand* by Steve Kowit (Tilbury House, 1995); *Orpheus and Company: Contemporary Poems on Greek Mythology,* Deborah De Nicola, ed. (University Press of New England Press, 1999); and *The Poetry of Men's Lives: An International Anthology,* Fred Moramarco and Al Zolynas, eds. (University of Georgia Press, 2004). My thanks also to those editors who subsequently republished some of these poems in other journals & anthologies. Finally, I extend my warmest thanks to Richard Mathews, editor-in-chief of University of Tampa Press, for his generous and invaluable assistance in editing and designing this book.

About the Author

Steve Kowit's collections of poetry include *Lurid Confessions* (Carpenter Press), *The Dumbbell Nebula* (Heyday Books) and, most recently, *The Gods of Rapture*, a collection of poems inspired by the erotic verse of India (City Works Press). His poetry has appeared in many journals and anthologies and a number of his poems have been read by Garrison Keillor on National Public Radio. His teaching manual, *In the Palm of Your Hand: The Poet's Portable Workshop* (Tilbury House), has gone through many printings and remains one of the most popular books on the subject. In addition to winning the 2006 Tampa Review Prize for Poetry for *The First Noble Truth*, he has been the recipient of a National Endowment Fellowship in Poetry, two Pushcart Prizes, and several other awards.

Kowit grew up in Brooklyn, New York, and then moved to San Francisco during that city's brief counterculture revolution. After refusing to serve in Vietnam he spent three years living in Mexico and Central and South America. Returning to the U.S., he worked as a book editor in Florida and then moved to San Diego, where he founded that city's first animal rights organization and became involved in the Zen, Vipassana, and Gurdjieff communities.

He has taught at colleges in Idaho and Maryland and at both the University of California, San Diego, and San Diego State University. He currently teaches at Southwestern College and lives in the backcountry hills of San Diego County near the Tecate, Mexico, border with his wife, Mary, and several animal companions.

About the Book

The First Noble Truth is set in New Caledonia types, based on the original 1938-39 Linotype designs by American typographer and graphic designer William A. Dwiggins. Taking his inspiration from Scotland, Dwiggins described his Caledonia (the Latin name for Scotland) as having "something of that simple, hard-working, feet-on-the-ground quality that has kept Scotch Roman in service for so many years." He also incorporated from Bulmer types a characteristic he described as "liveliness of action" and tried to embody "in the curves, the way they get away from the straight stems with a calligraphic flick, and in the nervous angle on the underside of the arches as they descend to the right." The book has been designed and typeset by Richard Mathews at the University of Tampa Press. It is printed on acid-free recycled text paper and bound in biodegradable Iris cloth in support of the Green Press Initiative by Thomson-Shore of Dexter, Michigan.

POETRY FROM THE UNIVERSITY OF TAMPA PRESS

Jenny Browne, *At Once*

Richard Chess, *Chair in the Desert*

Richard Chess, *Tekiah*

Richard Chess, *Third Temple*

Kevin Jeffery Clarke, *The Movie of Us*

Jane Ellen Glasser, *Light Persists**

Kathleen Jesme, *Fire Eater*

Steve Kowit, *The First Noble Truth**

Lance Larsen, *In All Their Animal Brilliance**

Julia B. Levine, *Ask**

Sarah Maclay, *Whore**

John Willis Menard, *Lays in Summer Lands*

Barry Silesky, *This Disease*

Jordan Smith, *For Appearances**

Jordan Smith, *The Names of Things Are Leaving*

Lisa M. Steinman, *Carslaw's Sequences*

Marjorie Stelmach, *A History of Disappearance*

Richard Terrill, *Coming Late to Rachmaninoff*

Matt Yurdana, *Public Gestures*

* Denotes winner of the Tampa Review Prize for Poetry